GALLUP GUIDES FOR YOUTH FACING PERSISTENT PREJUDICE

The LGBT Community

GALLUP GUIDES FOR YOUTH FACING PERSISTENT PREJUDICE

- Asians
- Blacks
- Hispanics
- Jews
- The LGBT Community
- Muslims
- Native North American Indians
- People with Mental and Physical Challenges

GALLUP GUIDES FOR YOUTH FACING PERSISTENT PREJUDICE

The LGBT Community

Jaime Seba

Mason Crest

Mason Crest
370 Reed Road
Broomall, Pennsylvania 19008
www.masoncrest.com

Printed and bound in the United States of America.

First printing
9 8 7 6 5 4 3 2 1

ISBN-13: 978-1-4222-2462-5 (hardcover series)
ISBN-13:978-1-4222-2467-0 (hardcover)
ISBN-13: 978-1-4222-9340-9 (e-book)
ISBN-13: 978-1-4222-2476-2 (paperback)

Library of Congress Cataloging-in-Publication Data

Seba, Jaime.
 Gallup guides for youth facing persistent prejudice. The LGBT community / by Jaime Seba.
     p. cm.
  title: LGBT community
 Includes bibliographical references and index.
  ISBN 978-1-4222-2467-0 (hbk.) -- ISBN 978-1-4222-2462-5 (series hbk.) -- ISBN 978-1-4222-2476-2 (pbk.) -- ISBN 978-1-4222-9340-9 (ebook)
  1. Homophobia--United States--Juvenile literature. 2. Gay youth--United States--Juvenile literature. 3. Sexual minorities--Civil rights--United States--Juvenile literature. I. Title. II. Title: LGBT community.
  HQ76.45.U5S43 2013
  306.76'60835--dc23
                                    2012017108

Produced by Harding House Publishing Services, Inc.
www.hardinghousepages.com
Interior design by Micaela Sanna.
Page design elements by Cienpies Design / Illustrations | Dreamstime.com.
Cover design by Torque Advertising + Design.

CONTENTS

What Is Prejudice?

The root word of prejudice is "pre-judge." Prejudiced people judge others based purely on the group to which they belong; they make assumptions about others that may have no basis in reality. They believe that if your skin is darker or you fall in love differently or wear different clothes or worship God in a different way, then they already know you are not as smart, not as nice, not as honest, not as valuable, or not as moral as they are. LGBT people have been the victim of prejudice for centuries.

Why do human beings experience prejudice? **Sociologists** believe humans have a basic tendency to fear anything that's unfamiliar or unknown. Someone who is strange (in that they're not like us) is scary; they're automatically dangerous or inferior. If we get to know the strangers, of course, we end up discovering that they're not so different from ourselves. They're not so frightening and threatening after all. But too often, we don't let that happen. We put up a wall between the strangers and ourselves. We're on the inside; they're on the

We often separate ourselves from those who are different. In many cases, this reaction is caused by fear.

The LGBT Community

outside. And then we peer over the wall, too far away from the people on the other side to see anything but our differences.

That's what has often happened when straight people have looked at the LGBT community. Instead of seeing all

What Does LGBT Mean?

It stands for lesbian (women who are sexually attracted to women), gay (usually men who are sexually attracted to men, but sometimes women homosexuals use this word for themselves as well), bisexual (individuals who are sexually attracted to members of both sexes), and transgender people (people who do not identify with their biological sex—in other words, a biologically male person whose identity is feminine, or a biologically female person whose identity is masculine). The term "LGBT" is an inclusive one that includes all four groups. Some people think it should be longer, to include more than four sexual variations. After all, human sexuality is sometimes complicated, and when we try to put it into categories, we end up with lots of variations. In response to that suggestion, however, one sociologist joked that we might as well use the entire alphabet, including "S" for straight.

High School Stereotypes

The average high school has its share of stereotypes—lumping a certain kind of person together, ignoring all the ways that each person is unique. These stereotypes are often expressed with a single word or phrase: "jock," "nerd," "goth," "prep," or "geek." The images these words call to mind are easily recognized and understood by others. But that doesn't mean they're true!

LGBT people as human beings, more like everyone else than they are different, straight people have often focused on the differences. And here's where another human tendency comes into play: stereotyping.

STEREOTYPES

A stereotype is a fixed, commonly held idea or image of a person or group that's based on an **oversimplification** of some observed or imagined trait. Stereotypes assume that whatever is believed about a group is typical for each and every individual within that group. "All blondes are dumb," is a stereotype. "Women are poor drivers," is another. "Men are slobs," is yet another, and "Gay men are **effeminate**," is one as well.

Many stereotypes tend to make us feel superior in some way to the person or group being stereotyped. Not all stereotypes are negative, however; some are positive—"Black men are good at basketball," "Gay guys have good fashion sense," or "Asian students are smart"—but that doesn't make them true. They ignore individuals' uniqueness. They make assumptions that may or may not be accurate.

We can't help our human tendency to put people into categories. As babies, we faced a confusing world filled with an amazing variety of new things. We needed a way to make sense

Group Pressure

Why do people continue to believe stereotypes despite evidence that may not support them? Researchers have found that it may have something to do with group pressure. During one experiment, seven members of a group were asked to state that a short line is longer than a long line. About a third of the rest of the group agreed that the short line was longer, despite evidence to the contrary. Apparently, people conform to the beliefs of those around them in order to gain group acceptance.

of it all, so one of our first steps in learning about the world around us was to sort things into separate slots in our heads: small furry things that said *meow* were kitties, while larger furry things that said a*rf-arf* were doggies; cars went *vroom-vroom*, but trains were longer and went *choo-choo*; little girls looked one way and little boys another; and doctors wore white coats, while police officers wore blue. These were our earliest stereotypes. They were a handy way to make sense of the world. They helped us know what to expect, so that each time we faced a new person or thing, we weren't starting all over again from scratch.

But stereotypes become dangerous when we continue to hold onto our mental images despite new evidence. (For instance, as a child you may have decided that all dogs bite—which means that when faced by friendly, harmless dogs, you assume they're dangerous and so you miss out on getting to know all dogs.) Stereotypes are particularly dangerous and destructive when they're directed at persons or groups of persons. That's when they turn into prejudice.

HOMOPHOBIA

Prejudice against LGBT people is often called homophobia, which means the fear and hatred of homosexuals. People who believe that it would be wrong to feel prejudice toward someone based on the color of her skin sometimes feel it's perfectly okay to have a negative attitude toward homosexuals. This giant blind spot in their thinking is based on the belief that homosexuality—unlike skin color—is a choice, and that the choice is wrong, unnatural, or sinful.

Everyone in the United States has the right to have their own religious beliefs. They're certainly entitled to make their own decisions about what is right and wrong. But unless

Not all churches reject homosexuals. Churches that display the Rainbow Flag proclaim their welcome to people in the LGBT community.

These protestors are members of the Westboro Church of Topeka, Kansas, which is an outspoken opponent of gay rights. Matthew Shepard, whom the protestors claim is in hell, was a young man who was murdered in a terrible hate crime.

people's actions are hurting others, none of us have the right to force our moral or religious beliefs on others. That goes against the ideas around which America is built.

Despite that, homophobia is a major problem in twenty-first century America. Some people are so filled with hate and fear that they commit crimes against people who belong to the LGBT community. They have even killed LGBT people.

These violent crimes that are inspired by prejudice are called "hate crimes." Tragically, in the United States, the number of hate crimes against LGBT people continues to rise. According to FBI statistics, well over a thousand such crimes were reported in 2009—but estimates for the actual number of violent crimes against people identified as LGBT are much higher. This is because many U.S. states do not legally recognize "gay hate crimes" as a separate category, and many gay people are, for many reasons, afraid to report these crimes.

At the same time that the LGBT community and their allies have been demanding—and slowly gaining—full legal and **civil rights**, their opponents on the religious and political **right** have been stepping up their organized efforts against gay rights, using the same homophobic language and arguments that have been used to **oppress** gay people for centuries.

History
Lesson

Ancient art (for example, the images of affectionate couples painted on Greek pottery and Egyptian walls thousands of years ago) and literature provide clear evidence that same-sex attraction and love has been around for a long, long time. Anthropologists, who study human societies around the world, have found same-sex behavior in just about all of them.

How Common Is Homosexuality?

Estimates vary as to the number of gay and lesbian people in the population, but many studies estimate that as many as 10 percent of American adults identify themselves as gay. That's one in ten people! To put it another way, about the same number of Americans are gay as are left-handed. (If you're gay and left-handed, you're a double minority.)

THE HISTORY OF HOMOPHOBIA

Prejudice against gay people has not existed in all times and places, however. Far from it. Among certain Native American tribes, "two-spirit people" (people who embodied both sexes) were highly respected as priests and healers. The early Christian Church, as uncovered by the research of Yale University historian John Boswell, had official rites for the blessing of gay marriages. And in much of modern Western Europe, gay

The Greek philosopher Plato discussed homosexual relationships. Such relationships were commonplace in ancient Greek society.

people have achieved full legal rights and full acceptance as respected members of their communities.

But homophobia runs deep in **Western culture** and in the Judeo-Christian and Islamic religious traditions. In the ancient legal code of the Jewish people, preserved in the Book of Leviticus in the Jewish and Christian Bible, a man "lying" with another man was punishable by death.

While ancient Rome was generally accepting of homosexuality, things changed under the influence of Christianity.

This drawing shows two male lovers being burned at the stake outside Zürich in 1482. Despite incidents like this, historians have recently discovered that a form of male same-sex marriage existed in medieval Europe.

The Emperor Constantius declared same-sex marriage illegal in the year 342, and the Christian emperors Valentian II, Theodosius I, and Arcadius declared homosexual sex to be illegal; those who were guilty of it were condemned to be publicly burned alive. The emperor Justinian (526–575) claimed that homosexuals were responsible for famines and earthquakes, just as the Romans had blamed Christians for all kinds of troubles in earlier centuries.

For the next thousand and more years, laws based on a particular **interpretation** of the Bible encouraged homophobia and hate crimes. While only enforced at certain times and in certain places, these laws brought people accused of homosexuality before the courts, with punishments ranging from jail sentences to public whippings to burning at the stake. Homosexuals were punished as criminals and sinners in old Europe in exactly the same way, and with the same Biblical authority, as were Jews and **heretics**. Meanwhile, great artists such as Leonardo da Vinci and Michelangelo, men who were making enormous contributions to art and culture during this era, may possibly have been homosexuals themselves.

The early settlers of America brought their traditions and their prejudices with them. Strict laws against same-sex behavior, including the death penalty, were enacted in the American colonies. **Sodomy** laws, applying equally to gay and to straight people but usually used only against gays, were put into effect (and many still remained on the books in many U.S. states in the twenty-first century).

With an increase in the understanding of scientific principles in the 1900s, what had been considered "sinful" behavior in the

The Stonewall Inn was raided by the police in 1969, setting off riots that eventually sparked the beginning of the Gay Pride movement. Today, the Stonewall Inn remains a symbol of pride to the LGBT community.

past (like being gay) began to be seen as a normal part of human behavior. Early sex researchers like Magnus Hirschfield (1868–1935) in Germany argued that since homosexual behavior was just another human activity and did not hurt other people, it was simply not logical—and was in fact, morally wrong—to punish it as a crime. Whether or not it was a "sin" was the problem of religious groups, Hirschfield believed, and should be completely separate from the concerns of government and law.

The **liberal** principles supported by the new science of psychology and the call for increasing human rights for minorities was making some progress in the fight for LGBT rights, especially in Europe—and then the Nazis came to power in Germany in the 1930s. Like Jews, gypsies, Communists, and other minorities, gay people were **persecuted** as "unfit to live" in Nazi-occupied Europe. Arrested and sent to concentration camps, thousands of gay people were executed or died from disease and starvation in the camps. They were forced to wear the pink triangle on their prison uniform that often set them apart for particularly brutal treatment.

And while American soldiers—quite a few of them gay and lesbian—had fought bravely in World War II (1939–1945) for the principles of human freedom, they returned home

Homosexuals in Nazi Germany

From the United States Holocaust Museum: Persecution of Homosexuals by the Nazis 1933–1945:

- Under Paragraph 175 of the criminal code, male homosexuality was illegal in Germany. The Nazis arrested an estimated 100,000 homosexual men, 50,000 of whom were imprisoned.
- During the Nazi regime, the police had the power to jail indefinitely—without trial—anyone they chose, including those deemed dangerous to Germany's moral fiber.
- Between 5,000 and 15,000 gay men were interred in concentration camps in Nazi Germany. These prisoners were marked by pink triangle badges and, according to many survivor accounts, were among the most abused groups in the camps.
- Nazis interested in finding a "cure" for homosexuality conducted medical experiments on some gay concentration camp inmates. These experiments caused illness, mutilation, and even death, and yielded no scientific knowledge.

to a country that was still racist, sexist, and homophobic. In the 1950s and '60s, men and women who gathered together in bars and clubs often faced police raids, arrest, and public exposure. People's personal lives and careers were destroyed simply for being caught dancing with a member of their own sex. Hate crimes against gay people—robbery, violence, and harassment—went unreported because of gay people's fear of public exposure and law enforcement's own homophobia. Religious leaders preached against homosexual "sinners," families disowned and rejected their own gay sons and lesbian daughters, and gay people were oppressed and humiliated by laws that excluded and denied them their basic rights and protections as citizens. Most gay people led lives of secrecy and denial in order to escape punishing social **stigma** and legal prosecution. The religious, legal, and medical **establishments** were united in their homophobia. In fact, homophobia was completely **institutionalized** in America. And it would take a strong and brave gay liberation movement, starting in the 1970s, to begin the long battle against institutionalized homophobia.

Today that battle is still going on.

Real-Life Stories

When country singer Chely Wright was sixteen, she knew she was a lesbian. She was mostly comfortable with her identity inside, but she believed she could never show it on the outside.

"For the most part, I knew, I guess I'm okay. But I also knew—you have to hide this because I'm either going to get the crap beaten out of me or I'm going to get in big trouble," she said. "And I know I'm not going to fit in school. . . . My band's not going to get hired. My dreams of country music wouldn't pan out."

Chely came close to ending her life, but instead she experienced a rebirth, realizing that she can be accepted by both God and herself.

As Chely's career progressed, she had public relationships with men and kept her gay life hidden. For years, she struggled with trying to find happiness when she had to deny such an important part of herself. Even though she had commercial success, earning an Academy of Country Music Award and nominations for three Country Music Association Awards, she was depressed about the piece of her life that was missing.

Then, when she was nearly forty, she found herself standing in her home, staring at herself in the mirror. She had a gun in her mouth, and she was ready to pull the trigger.

"At that moment, I was looking at myself and feeling like I was outside of my body, watching somebody do something that I had made such a harsh judgment about my entire life," she said. "I had been so critical of people who had committed suicide; I judged them for being God-less and weak. And I was watching that in the mirror and realizing, 'Holy crap! That's me.'

"But as I was about to pull the trigger, I realized I wasn't crying. And I was shocked: Shouldn't I be crying? Don't people cry when they kill themselves? Isn't it supposed to be more emotional than this?

"And as I was about to pull my thumb back and do it, I said a prayer to God to forgive me for what I was about to do because I know the gift of life is the most precious thing. And I had some things in my life that kind of flashed through my brain and one of them was sunlight and I thought about my dogs and I thought about music and how much I love music. And I thought about a kiss from my partner, my ex-partner— the only love in my life I'd ever known—and I heard a noise and it was the sound of my heart pounding in my head.

Today, Chely Wright is proud to claim her identity as a gay woman.

"And I looked up in the mirror again and my eyes were just welled up with tears and my cheeks were wet and tears were streaming down. I could barely even see. I couldn't focus because there were so many tears coming out of my eyes. And the dam broke. And my emotions enveloped me and I became one with myself again. I got back into my body. I was no longer outside of my body watching this cold person—this human with a gun in her mouth. I didn't know that I wasn't going to—on the next day—kill myself. I knew on that night I wouldn't do it."

Though Wright was tempted to take such a drastic action again, instead she began to accept who she really was. She decided to come out publicly in 2010, a move that she believes set her free and gave her a sort of re-birth in her life.

Prejudice and Self-Esteem

When your identity causes you to face prejudice from many of the people around you, it's hard to feel good about yourself. The loss of self-worth can make it hard to be strong emotionally and psychologically. Many LGBT people struggle with depression as a result. And for thousands of LGBT people, suicide seems like the only option when they are faced with the immense struggles and stress of understanding and accepting their sexual orientation.

As part of the normal experience of growing up, many teenagers encounter significant feelings of stress, confusion and self-doubt. These intense feelings can be overwhelming for any adolescent, which is why suicide is the third leading cause of death among all young people ages fifteen to twenty-four. And these emotions are often much more challenging for LGBT kids, especially if they don't have the resources or support necessary to help them. Studies have shown that LGBT young people who do not receive support from their families

"Coming out of the closet" can be a scary thing for a teenager to do, since it often means risking rejection from friends, family, and the larger community. But hiding your true self can be just as dangerous to your mental health.

are more than eight times more likely to attempt suicide than straight kids their same age.

Much research has been done to determine exactly why this is the case. The increased number of suicide attempts among LGBT people is not because of their sexual orientation itself. In other words, feeling suicidal is not part of being gay or the result of coming out. Instead, these feelings can come as a response to being bullied at school, being treated poorly at home or in a religious community, or feeling as if they have failed to live up to expectations of being "normal."

Being gay or lesbian isn't something individuals can control or change. So when LGBT people hear their friends or families make jokes about other gay people, it can have a strong and lasting impression. Likewise, when people questioning their sexuality believe that others will not accept them if they are gay, they are more inclined to hide their feelings.

When anyone is told they are bad or wrong because of whom they are, that trauma and stress can lead to mental health issues such as depression or anxiety. This is frequently what happens to LGBT people and others who are considered different from their **peers**, putting them at risk for suicide.

Depression is a medical condition. Individuals suffering from depression may constantly feel sad or tense.

What Causes Homosexuality?

Trying to answer this question is part of a major debate in science that has been going on for many years, the debate over "nature versus nurture." The nature side of the debate would be supported if it could be proven that gay people are *born* gay, that being gay is a biological trait like the color of a person's skin. The nurture side says that it is the way a person is raised, his relationship with his parents and his environment that makes him *become* gay. Or could it be, as some people believe, that certain people simply make a *choice* to be gay? The issues these questions raise are very important to the LGBT community's continuing struggle for full civil rights and acceptance and a part of *every* person's, straight or gay, desire to understand themselves and who they are.

Scientists have discovered that same-sex sexual behavior is very common in the animal kingdom, of which human beings are a part. Homosexuality has been observed in close to 1500 species and is well documented in over five hundred, including black swans, mallard ducks, and penguins, all the apes, elephants, giraffes, sheep, hyenas, lizards, and even fruit flies! Same-sex penguin pairs mate for life and sometimes even raise orphaned chicks together. Researcher Petter Bóckman has written, "No species has been found in which homosexual behavior has *not* been shown to exist, with the exception of species that never have sex at all, such as sea urchins." While some homophobic people say that homosexuality is a "crime against nature," nature seems to feel differently!

In the end, though, does it really matter what causes homosexuality? Being gay is really all about whom a person loves, isn't it? Even if you don't happen to agree with a person's choice in this most personal and private matter, do you have the right to deny another person's happiness? Does America have the right to deny up to 10 percent of its citizens their full legal and civil rights because the majority doesn't approve of their lifestyle?

What do you think?

"At first I was feeling sad all the time, even though I had no reason to be," said Rob, who shared his experience with depression on the resource website 4therapy.com. "Then the sadness turned into anger, and I started having fights with my family and friends. I felt really bad about myself, like I wasn't good enough for anyone. It got so bad that I wished I would go to bed and never wake up."

People struggling with depression often lose energy and feel sad, restless, or tired all the time. In some cases, this can lead to thinking that suicide is the only option or the only way to fix a very difficult situation.

Parents, family members, and friends also need to be able to recognize the signs of depression. In Rob's case, his brother noticed that his behavior changed and immediately suggested that Rob see a doctor. Rob did, and he learned that depression is a real illness. It's not something that can be fixed by being told to just "cheer up!" Like all medical problems, the most effective treatment will come from a doctor or other health-care professional. Rob began seeing a therapist, who helped him talk through his problems.

"This treatment helps me control depression in my everyday life," he said. "It has taken some time, but I'm finally feeling like myself again."

People who don't understand that depression is an illness often seek cures or treatments that may seem to work in the short term by dulling the pain—such as drugs or alcohol—but that won't provide the real support and attention that individuals suffering from depression actually need. In fact, alcohol itself is a depressant; in the long run, it just makes people who are depressed feel even worse.

In a similar way, when parents, friends and other family members don't understand what it means to be LGBT, they often look for some type of treatment or cure that will make people straight. While people may be able to change the way they behave, experts explain that a person's identity on the inside isn't something that can be removed or made different. And often attempting to do this can do much more harm than good.

All this also can increase feelings of depression and isolation. When people reach the point of feeling hopeless enough to consider suicide, there are often outward signs and indicators. They may see themselves as bad or inferior people, and tell their friends about those feelings. Suicidal teens may also withdraw from their friends, spend time alone, abuse drugs and alcohol, and lose interest in things they usually enjoy.

Any statements a person makes that suggest she may be considering suicide should always be taken seriously. Sometimes just talking about the issues—whether with a parent, friend, or mental health professional—can be very helpful. The key is to not ignore these feeling and to seek help as soon as possible.

"Suicide is truly a permanent solution to a temporary problem," said Ashley Albright, who works for a suicide prevention program. "Although we can give you the number of completed and attempted suicides throughout the past decade, there is no way we can give how many times someone took the opportunity to listen, care—and a life was saved."

BULLYING

When Anna Rangos walked down the halls of her high school, she frequently heard homophobic slurs from her classmates. Eventually, it became so bad that she brought the issue to her district's school board in May of 2010.

"My self-esteem just totally dropped because of what was being said. Every single year, there's an incident, and I've never seen a kid punished," she said. "After a while, it's so frustrating, it hurts a lot to have people say those things to you while not having people who are supposed to protect you do that."

In most American high schools, bullying isn't limited to lesbian, gay, bisexual, and transgender students. According to the National Center for Educational Statistics, about one in three students (about one-third or 30 percent) between the ages of twelve and eighteen reported being bullied in school in 2009. Eight years earlier, only 14 percent of that population said they had experienced bullying.

But for LGBT students, this type of harassment can be even more damaging because it reinforces feelings of confusion or loneliness they may already have because they are different from most of their classmates.

Bullying has been cited as a probable contributor to many teen suicides, including high-profile cases in 2009 involving students as young as eleven years old. This has led to a heightened awareness for educators and parents about the effects of bullying.

At Rangos' high school, there is a Gay-Straight Alliance. But she said many of her classmates didn't participate in the group because they were afraid of being labeled and harassed by other students. When she listened to the way other students in her school spoke, she often heard anti-gay statements that made her feel bad about herself, even when that may not have been the intention.

That can lead to something called internalized homophobia—when LGBT people think negatively about themselves and their lives because of all the bad things they hear other people say about gay people. In other words, homophobia isn't just something they face in the outside world—they also carry it around inside themselves. This often keeps LGBT people from coming out, and instead they feel the need to keep their sexual orientation a secret. In many cases, they may even actively try to hide who they are because they are afraid.

"When I first got to Nashville . . . I worked at a theme park called Opryland and there were gay boys in my cast," said Chely Wright. "I don't know that there were any gay girls. But I was fully aware that I was gay, of course, and I was very sure that God was okay with me. Yet I slung daggers of hatred toward the gay boys because I was so afraid that they might identify something in me that would be some identifying factor—that they might be able to know that I was gay and I wanted to throw them off in case they thought I might be."

That reaction is not at all uncommon, especially among people like Wright who have strong religious beliefs. She told the boys what they did was disgusting. These were the messages that she had heard from her church and other people in her life.

As Wright got older and understood more about herself, she saw that this was her own internalized homophobia. She was so frightened of other people's reaction to her that she attacked other people who were like her. After she came out, she said this was something she strongly regretted.

"When I would go into Tower Records in Nashville, I was recognized by the young kids that worked at the record store," she said. "In fact, they would bring records or posters for me to sign. And I was a fan of kd lang's music. But when she came out, I wouldn't purchase a kd lang or Melissa Etheridge [another openly gay musician] record in Nashville because I was afraid for them to see me buying it. That comes with a great deal of shame for me to admit. I'm embarrassed to admit that—but that's how deep the fear and pain went."

When a fellow singer asked Wright directly if she was gay, she denied it. In that moment, she realized something in her life had to change. She didn't believe that being gay was a sin, but she believed that lying was. And for the first time, instead of just hiding who she was, she had clearly lied about it.

This helped her decide to come out to the world in 2010. She didn't want to be one of those people who said one thing in public, but did something else in their real lives. She recognized that same behavior in other high-profile people, such as politicians and religious leaders, who would publicly say bad things about the LGBT community, while privately they were actually gay.

"I felt it was really important for me to stand up and admit that because it is so **prevalent** in our culture, in American society," she said. "Because we've got people writing legislation and people in public office, people in powerful positions who have the chance and the opportunity to write policy who are signing paperwork that goes against the gay community and they themselves are **closeted**. And I thought it was really important that I say, 'Pay attention to those who are the most vocal against gays and lesbians because I can tell you—those who spew the most venom, pay attention to that.' Because I did it."

"Gays, lesbians, and bisexuals still face discrimination on a number of fronts," said Dr. Elaine Zahnd, one of the lead researchers who worked on the UCLA study. "Some heterosexuals seek to **stigmatize** and isolate gays, lesbians, and bisexuals. Stigma and social isolation may result in lower self-esteem and increase one's **vulnerability** to abuse."

Zahnd's research team also found that nearly one in ten people who reported violence in their relationships also engaged in binge drinking. This is most likely a way to cope with the abuse, which many people feel they deserve, because they think of themselves as being worthless or hopeless.

Researchers at the Family Acceptance Project at San Francisco State University studied the impact of rejection or acceptance of LGBT people by their families. What the researchers found was that the people who reported high levels of rejection from their families during adolescence were eight times more likely to have attempted suicide by

In 2011, New York State passed a law that allowed same sex couples to be legally married. Gay rights advocates saw this as a huge step forward in the battle against prejudice.

HIV/AIDS and Homosexuality

In many places around the world, including the United States, people think that HIV/AIDS is a "gay disease." People who have HIV/AIDS are sometimes rejected and discriminated against; some have lost their jobs or been the victims of violence. The stigma that's been attached to HIV/AIDS has kept many people from seeking HIV testing—or from being treated, once they've received a diagnosis. This can turn what might otherwise being a manageable chronic disease into a death sentence.

In many developed countries, there is an association between AIDS and homosexuality or bisexuality, and this association goes along with higher levels of homosexual prejudice. However, in the developing world, such as many nations in Africa, HIV/AIDS is more common among heterosexuals. This is because risky sexual behaviors, whether heterosexual or homosexual, put you at risk of getting HIV/AIDS.

age twenty-five. They were also nearly six times more likely to have serious issues with depression, and their risk for drug abuse and contracting sexually transmitted diseases was three times higher than the overall population.

Prejudice is destructive, no matter who it's directed against. It hurts communities and it hurts individuals. Many people are fighting homophobia and other forms of prejudice—but they need your help!

Fighting Prejudice

Young people, both gay and straight, are growing up in a world where the full social acceptance of LGBT people is advancing with an energy never seen before in history. Opinion polls indicate that young people support gay rights issues such as same-sex marriage and adoption rights in numbers far greater than their parents' and grandparents' generations. And positive gay models are everywhere: in the sports and entertainment industry, in politics and religion, in your neighborhood, in your classroom, and in your family. Teenagers are coming out as gays or lesbians in large numbers, supported by Gay-Straight Alliances and anti-homophobia education programs in many schools. In many ways, this may be the best time ever to be an LGBT kid!

And yet we know that middle schools and high schools are not easy places to be different. Peer pressure dominates the social world of adolescents. Teenagers have always split themselves into groups: the popular kids, the jocks, the science nerds, the partiers. A strong loyalty to your particular group is a big part of being a teenager. One group can decide it dislikes another group. Gossip can hurt people. And nothing hurts a young person more than rejection by their peers.

Studies show that LGBT kids still have it rough. One study of 192 gay teenage boys found that one-third of them reported being verbally abused by one or more family members when they came out, and another 10 percent reported being physically assaulted. In a nationwide study of over 9,000 gay high school students, 24 percent of the boys reported being **victimized**, verbally or physically at least ten times in the previous school year because of their sexual orientation; 11 percent of lesbians reported the same thing. Gay teenagers are four times more likely to be threatened with a deadly weapon than their straight peers. Teenage victims of homophobia often experience severe depression, a sense of helplessness, low self-esteem, and even suicidal thoughts (LGBT teenagers are almost five times more likely to attempt suicide than straight teenagers). And the negative family, school, and social pressures gay teenagers face can lead them to abuse

Gay pride is a movement that affirms LGBT identity. It has three main premises: that people should be proud of their sexual orientation and gender identity, that diversity is a gift, and that sexual orientation and gender identity are inherent and cannot be intentionally altered.

drugs and alcohol, engage in unsafe sexual activity, and have body image and eating disorders. Not a pretty picture, is it?

If you're a straight teenager, are you contributing to the unhappiness and insecurity, physically and emotionally, of gay and lesbian kids in your school and community? Are YOU homophobic? Ask yourself:

- Do I have negative stereotypes of gay people?
- Do I participate in bullying or making fun of gay kids in my school, or allow it to happen even if I think it's wrong?
- Do I use hurtful language (like "fag" or "dyke") when talking about gay people? Or use the word "gay" in a negative way to mean something uncool?
- Do I tell **offensive** jokes about gay and lesbian people? Or laugh at them?
- Do I *not* treat gay and lesbian people with the same polite- ness and respect that I expect from other people?

If you answered "yes" to any of these questions, you may have to admit to yourself that you are homophobic, and that your dislike or fear of LGBT people is a part of an unfair system that oppresses and excludes people just because of who they are, and who they happen to want to love.

CELEBRATING DIVERSITY

If you want to fight prejudice, one of the first things that has to change is the way you think and talk about differences. Instead of being frightened of the ways people are different from you, you need to start feeling curious and interested. You need to be willing to learn from people who are different. You need to enjoy the differences!

Most people enjoy **diversity** when it comes to the world around them. You probably like different kinds of food. You read different kinds of books. You enjoy different kinds of music and television shows. The world would be pretty boring if everything was exactly the same!

People are also diverse, in the same way as the rest of the world is. Although all of us feel the same basic emotions—sadness and happiness, anger and laughter, loneliness and pride, jealousy and compassion, to name just a few—and most of us have pretty much the same structure—a head, a body, arms and legs—we also are different in many ways. Our hair, eyes, and skin come in different colors. Our noses are big or little or something in between. Our bodies are different sizes and shapes. And when you get down to the details—to our fingerprints and the DNA inside our cells—we're absolutely

Each human fingerprint is completely unique. As human beings, we are both all the same and all different from one another.

unique, despite all the things we have in common with other human beings. Each of us looks at the world a little differently. We believe different things. And we offer different things as well.

The world is a richer place because of all this human diversity. You can learn from and enjoy your friends because, although they're like you in some ways, they're also different from you in other ways. Those differences make them interesting! And in a similar way, we can learn from human beings' different

What Is the Golden Rule?

"Treat others the way you want to be treated." It's the most basic of all human moral laws—and it's been found in all religions and all cultures for thousands of years. The earliest record of this principle is in the Code of Hammurabi, written nearly 4,000 years ago. About 2,500 years ago, Confucius, the great Chinese philosopher, wrote, "Never impose on others what you would not choose for yourself." An ancient Egyptian papyrus contains a similar thought: "That which you hate to be done to you, do not do to another." Ancient Greek philosophers wrote, "Do not do to others what would anger you if done to you by others." An early Buddhist teacher expressed a similar concept: "Just as I am so are they, just as they are so am I." Jesus Christ, whom Christians follow, said, "Do unto others as you would have them do unto you." The Prophet Mohammed, whose teachings Muslims follow, said, "As you would have people do to you, do to them; and what you dislike to be done to you, don't do to them," as well as, "That which you seek for yourself, seek for all humans."

You can't follow this ancient rule and practice prejudice. The Golden Rule and prejudice are not compatible!

languages, different music, different ways of thinking about God, different lifestyles.

Prejudice, however, focuses on the differences in a negative way. It doesn't value all that differences have to offer us. Instead, it divides people into in-groups and out-groups. It breaks the Golden Rule.

RECOGNIZING PREJUDICE

Do you recognize prejudice when you hear it? Sometimes it's hard. We get so used to certain ways of thinking that we become blind to what's really going on. But anytime you hear people being lumped together, chances are prejudice is going on. Statements like these are all signs of prejudice:

Poor kids smell bad.
Girls run funny.
Old people are boring.
Special ed kids are weird.
Jocks are jerks.

Rather than building bridges between people, prejudice puts up walls. It makes it hard to talk to others or understand them. And those walls can lead to hatred, violence, and even wars.

A first step to ending prejudice is speaking up against it whenever you hear it. Point it out when you hear your friends or family being prejudiced. They may not even realize that's what they're being.

But even more important, you need to spot prejudice when it's inside you. That's not always easy, of course. Here are some ways experts suggest you can fight prejudice when you find it inside yourself:

1. Learn more about groups of people who are different from you. Read books about their history; read fiction that allows you to walk in their shoes in your imagination; watch movies that portray them accurately.

2. Get to know people who are different from you. Practice being a good listener, focusing on what they have to say rather than on your own opinions and experiences. Ask about others' backgrounds and family stories.

3. Practice compassion. Imagine what it would feel like to be someone who is different from you. Your imagination is a powerful tool you can use to make the world better!

Fighting Prejudice

4. Believe in yourself. Surprisingly, a lot of the time, psychologists say, prejudice is caused by having a bad self-concept. If you don't like who you are and you don't believe

Today, Gay Pride parades are taking place around the world. This one was in Tel Aviv, Israel.

That's So Gay

The use of "gay" as a negative adjective is an increasingly common practice in American culture. Many children and adults use the term to refer to anything bad, weak, or otherwise undesirable. Although kids may not have bad intentions when they say it, such language only reinforces the idea that "gay" = "bad." Also, the language can do significant damage to gay and lesbian students, who are forced to endure such language with little recourse.

in your own abilities, you're more likely to be scared and threatened by others. People who are comfortable with themselves are also more comfortable with people who are different from themselves.

What does it all come down to in the end? Perhaps the war against prejudice can best be summed up with just two words—communication and respect.

FIND OUT MORE

In Books

Aldrich, Robert. *Gay Life & Culture: A World History.* New York: Rizzoli, 2006.

Fishbein, Harold D. *Peer Prejudice and Discrimination: The Origins of Prejudice.* Mahwah, N.J.: Lawrence Erlbaum, 2002.

Huegel, Kelly. *GLBTQ: The Survival Guide for Queer and Questioning Teens.* Minneapolis, Minn.: Free Spirit Publishing, 2003.

Pascoe, D. J. *Dude, You're a Fag: Masculinity and Sexuality in High School.* Berkeley: University of California Press: 2003.

On the Internet

THE GAY-STRAIGHT ALLIANCE NETWORK
gsanetwork.org

HIGH SCHOOL STUDENTS EXPLORE
EFFECTS OF HOMOPHOBIA
blog.mattalgren.com/2009/01/high-school-students-explore-
effects-homophobia

HISTORY OF THE GAY RIGHTS MOVEMENT IN THE U.S.
WWW.lifeintheusa.com/people/gaypeople.htm

HOMOPHOBIA IN SCHOOLS
www.365gay.com/news/homophobia-in-schools-remains-
major-problem

NAZI PERSECUTION OF HOMOSEXUALITY
www.ushmm.org/museum/exhibit/online/hsx

GLOSSARY

civil rights: The rights of a citizen to personal and political freedom under the law.

closeted: Not yet openly admitted one's sexual identity to friends, family, and the world at large.

diversity: Being different in lots of different ways.

effeminate: Possessing feminine qualities; usually applied to males in a negative way.

establishment: The people who hold influence and power in society.

heretics: People who disagree with the religious establishment; in the past they were often punished for their beliefs.

institutionalized: When ideas and ways of doing things that are accepted without question by the majority of people.

interpretation: A particular understanding of something.

liberal: Open to new ideas that support social change.

offensive: Hurtful to other people's feelings, embarrassing them, or encouraging negative stereotypes.

oppress: To keep another person, or a group of people, in an inferior position.

60

oversimplification: The process of making something complicated too simple.

peers: The people who are the same age as you are.

persecuted: Mistreated and oppressed.

prevalent: Common, occurring often.

right: In politics and religion, the right is the side that is generally against social change and new ideas; a word with a similar meaning is "conservative."

sociologists: People who study the way groups of humans behave.

sodomy: Any human sexual act that is not oriented toward reproduction is considered sodomy, but the term has often been used specifically for homosexual behaviors.

stigma: A mark of shame.

stigmatize: To put a mark of shame on someone or something.

victimized: Experienced unfair and negative treatment, like violence or bullying.

vulnerability: A state where one can be easily hurt.

Western culture: The civilization of Europe and the countries (the United States, Australia, Canada, etc.) most influenced by Europe.

BIBLIOGRAPHY

Aldrich, Robert. *Gay Life & Culture: A World History.* New York: Rizzoli, 2006.

Beck, Melinda. "What to Say When Your Teenager Says She's Gay." *The Wall Street Journal,* May 11, 2010.

DiFilippo, Dana. "Experts Puzzled, Worried by Youngsters' Suicides." *Philadelphia Daily News,* May 16, 2010.

Echegaray, Chris. "Christian Star Jennifer Knapp Lets Go, Comes Out." *The Tennessean,* May 9, 2010.

Fishbein, Harold D. *Peer Prejudice and Discrimination: The Origins of Prejudice.* Mahwah, N.J.: Lawrence Erlbaum, 2002.

Johnson, Ramon. "How Many Gay People Are There? Gay Population Statistics." About.com Guide, gaylife.about.com/od/comingout/a/population.htm (15 June 2010).

Kennedy, Hubert. "Karl Heinrich Ulrichs: Pioneer of the Modern Gay Movement." Peremptory Publications, 2002.

Ocamb, Karen. "Country Star Chely Wright Comes Out, Talks About Suicide, God, Melissa, kd and the Indigo Girls." *The Huffington Post,* May 6, 2010.

Ollove, Michael. "Bullying and Teen Suicide: How Do We Adjust School Climate?" *Christian Science Monitor,* April 28, 2010.

Rogers, Jack. *Jesus, the Bible, and Homosexuality.* Louisville, Ken.: Westminster John Knox Press, 2009.

Staff. "Student Seeks Greater Consequences for Harassment of Gay Students." *Niles Herald-Spectator*, May 10, 2010.

"Teen Suicide." *American Academy of Child & Adolescent Psychiatry*, May 2008.

INDEX

Picture Credits

About the Author

Jaime A. Seba studied political science at Syracuse University before switching her focus to communications. She has worked both in New York and on the West Coast as an activist for LGBT awareness. She is currently a freelance writer based in Seattle.